THE VOYNICH MANUSCRIPT

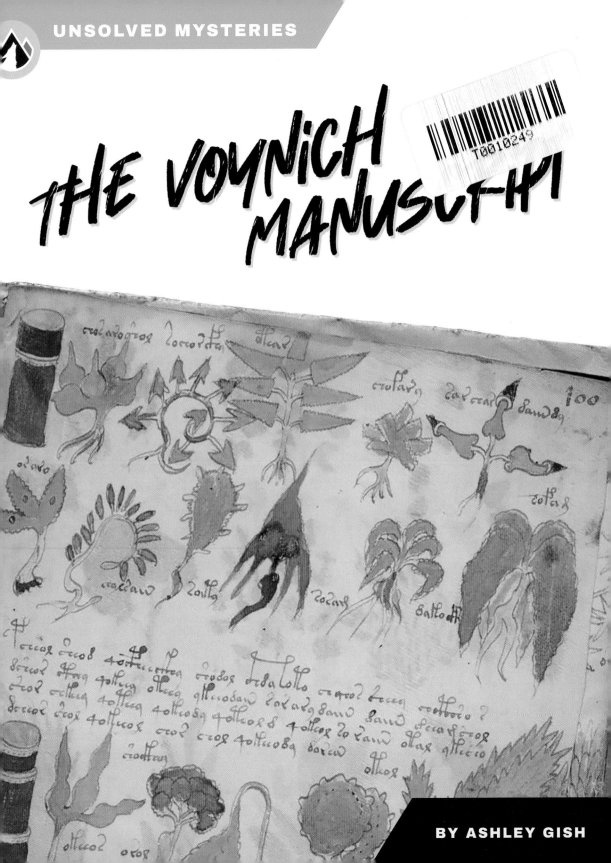

BY ASHLEY GISH

Apex is distributed by North Star Editions:
sales@northstareditions.com | 888-417-0195

Produced for Apex by Red Line Editorial.

Photographs ©: Beinecke Rare Book and Manuscript Library/Yale University/Wikimedia, cover, 1, 4–5, 14–15, 16–17, 18, 19, 20–21, 22–23, 24, 25, 26, 29; Wikimedia, 6, 10–11; Shutterstock Images, 9; Michael Maier/Library of Congress, 12; Leonardo da Vinci/Library of Congress, 13 (top); Cosomo Colombini/Library of Congress, 13 (bottom)

Library of Congress Control Number: 2022911839

ISBN
978-1-63738-437-4 (hardcover)
978-1-63738-464-0 (paperback)
978-1-63738-516-6 (ebook pdf)
978-1-63738-491-6 (hosted ebook)

Printed in the United States of America
Mankato, MN
012023

NOTE TO PARENTS AND EDUCATORS

Apex books are designed to build literacy skills in striving readers. Exciting, high-interest content attracts and holds readers' attention. The text is carefully leveled to allow students to achieve success quickly. Additional features, such as bolded glossary words for difficult terms, help build comprehension.

TABLE OF CONTENTS

CHAPTER 1

A MYSTERIOUS BOOK

n 1912, a man visited a school in Italy. He looked through the school's books. One manuscript looked odd. Its pages had colorful drawings and strange words.

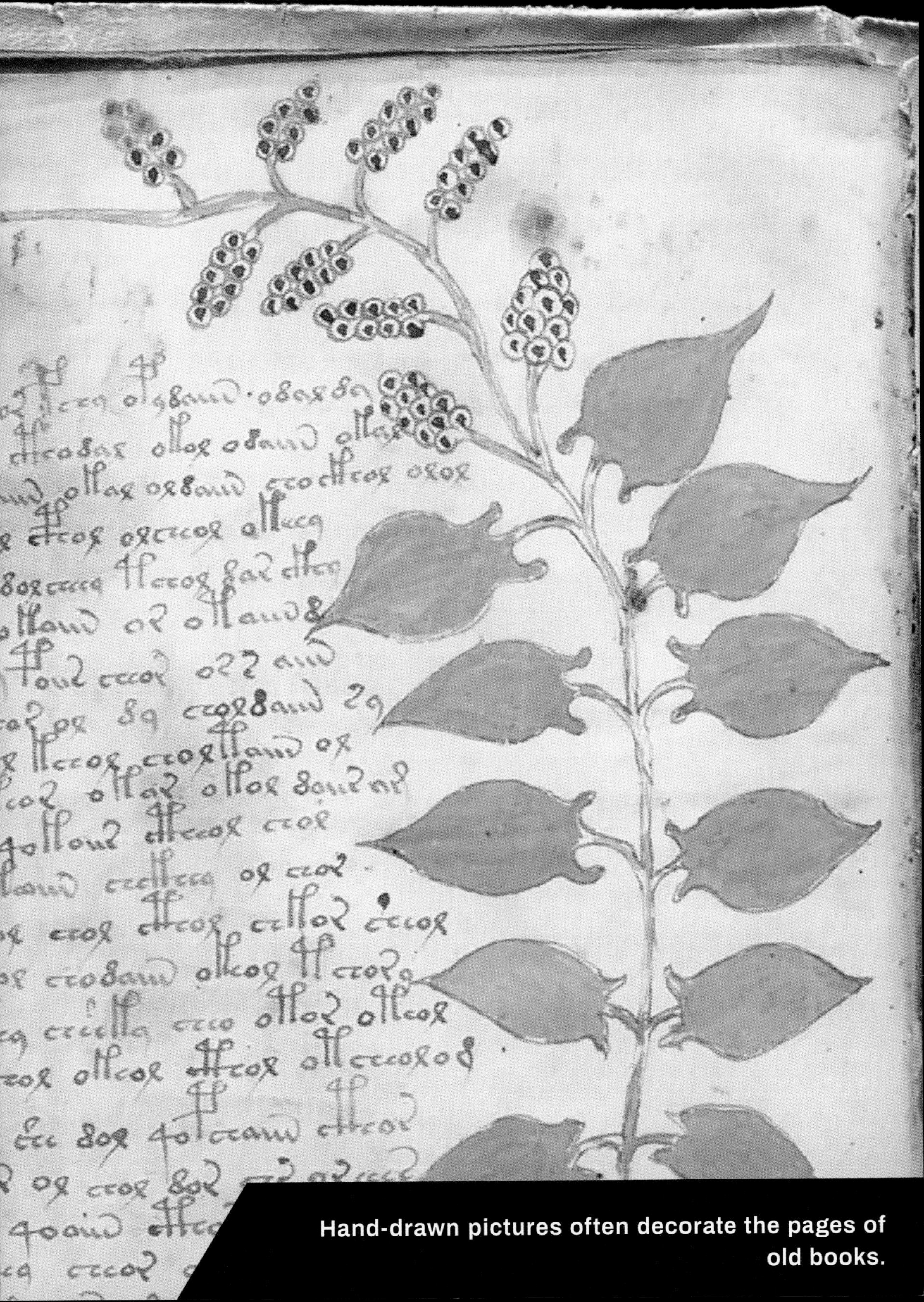

Hand-drawn pictures often decorate the pages of old books.

The man had never seen this language before. He bought the book. The man's name was Wilfrid Voynich. So, the book became known as the Voynich Manuscript.

COLLECTING BOOKS

Wilfrid Voynich owned bookstores. He bought and sold rare books. Sometimes he traveled to find them. Once, he crossed a desert in Mongolia.

 Wilfrid Voynich started bookstores in New York and London.

Voynich tried to translate the strange words. But he was not successful. He died in 1930. Since then, other people have tried to guess who wrote the book and what it says.

FAST FACT

Today, the Voynich Manuscript is in a library at Yale University.

Yale's Beinecke Rare Book and Manuscript Library has many old and valuable books.

CHAPTER 2

A SECRET PAST

Wilfrid Voynich wouldn't say where he got the book. Some people thought he made it to trick people. But after he died, his wife said he got it from Italy.

Voynich thought the manuscript might be about magic or science.

Roger Bacon lived in England in the 1200s.

People tried to guess the book's author. Some thought it was Roger Bacon. He studied alchemy. But experts don't think it was him.

NOT DA VINCI

Leonardo da Vinci was a great artist. He filled many notebooks with ideas and drawings. Some people thought he wrote the manuscript. But he lived after it was made.

Many of Leonardo da Vinci's notebooks have drawings and plans for inventions.

Leonardo da Vinci lived from 1452 to 1519.

In 2009, tests showed the manuscript was made in the 1400s. Experts believe it came from Europe. Not much else is known about it.

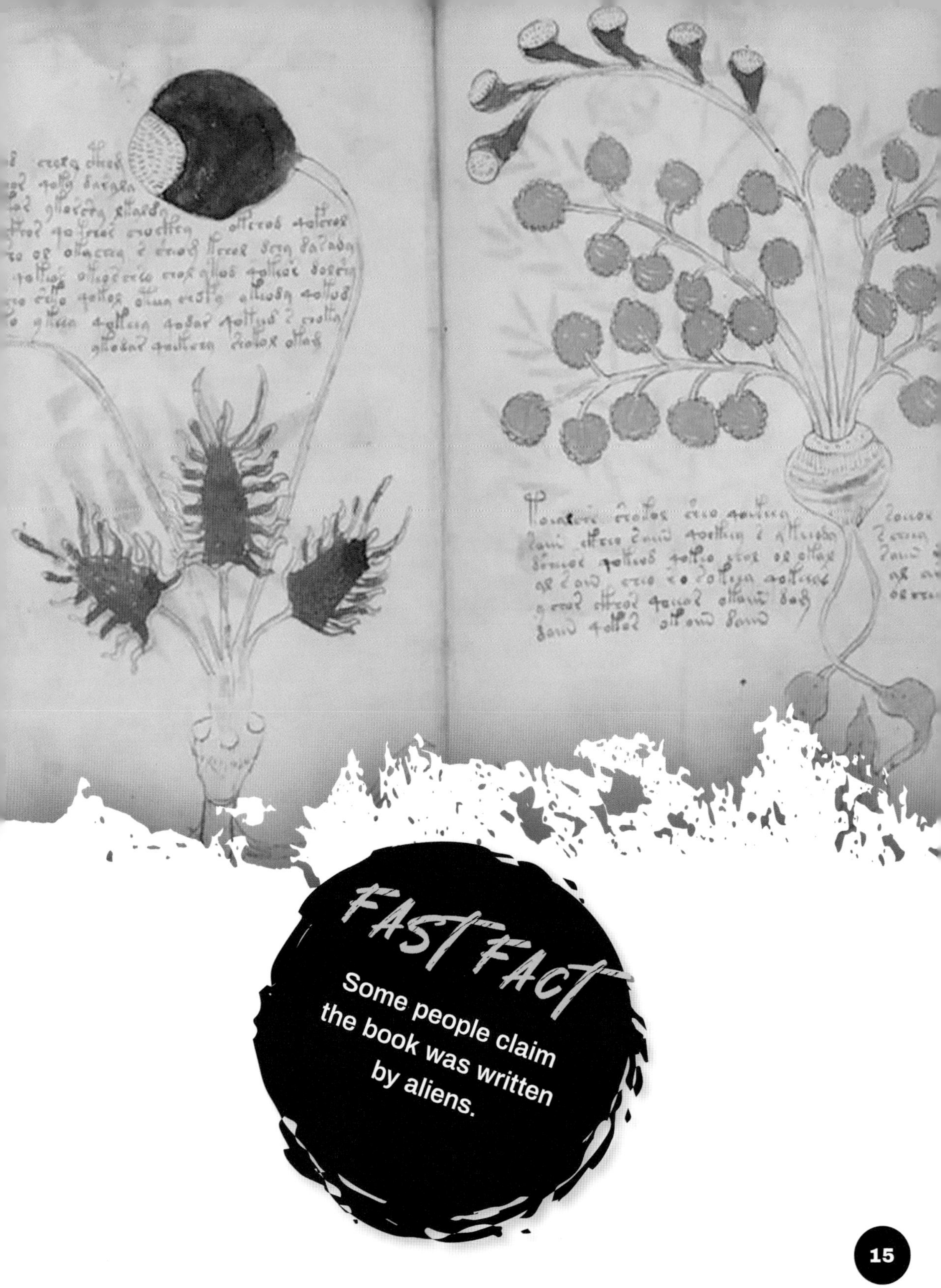

FAST FACT

Some people claim the book was written by aliens.

CHAPTER 3

STRANGE PAGES

The Voynich Manuscript has more than 240 pages. The pages are made of **vellum**. People can't read the words. But based on the pictures, they think the book has six parts.

The Voynich Manuscript's pages are about 9 inches (23 cm) tall and 6 inches (16 cm) wide.

Experts recognize some of the plants in the book. Others are unknown.

One section shows plants. Other parts look like astronomy, cosmology, recipes, or medicine. There's a section about the human body, too.

INVESTIGATING INK

The book uses several types of inks and paints. Scientists tested them to find what they were made of. They also learned the writer likely used a quill pen.

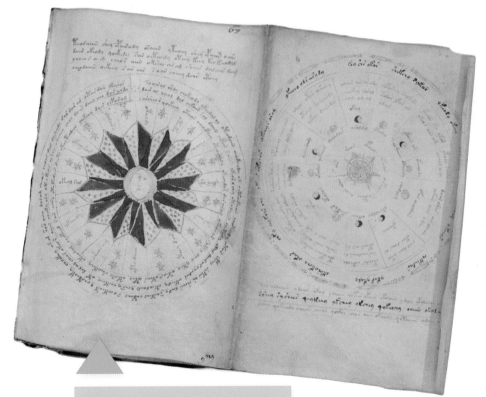

Some pages have charts that seem to show seasons and planets.

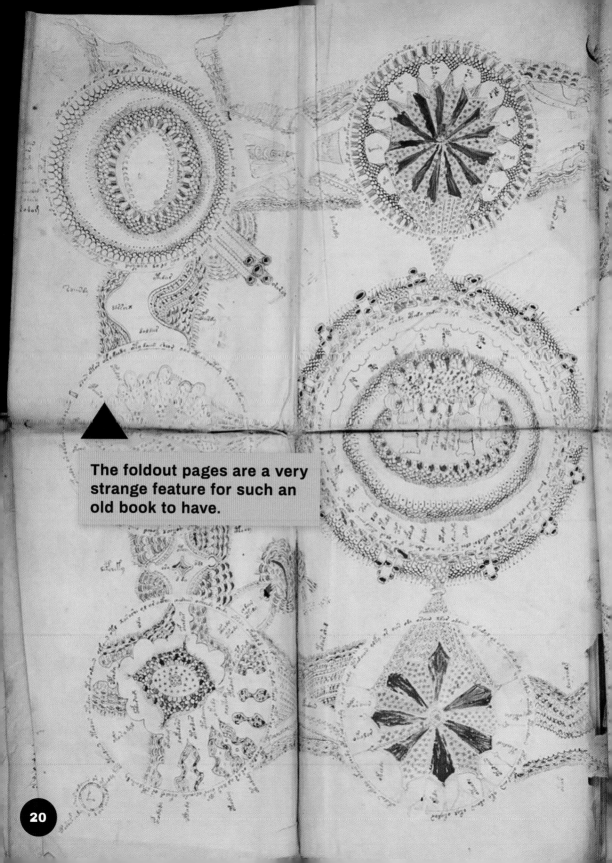

The foldout pages are a very strange feature for such an old book to have.

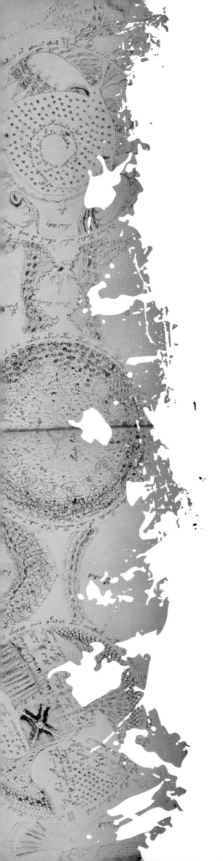

Some of the book's pages fold out. One large page shows buildings, stars, and a castle. Some people believe it's a map.

FAST FACT

Scientists think making the book likely took several months.

CHAPTER 4

AN UNKNOWN CODE?

Experts aren't sure what language the Voynich Manuscript uses. Some people think it's a form of Latin. Others say it's Hebrew.

The book's writing looks similar to English. But it has some extra letters.

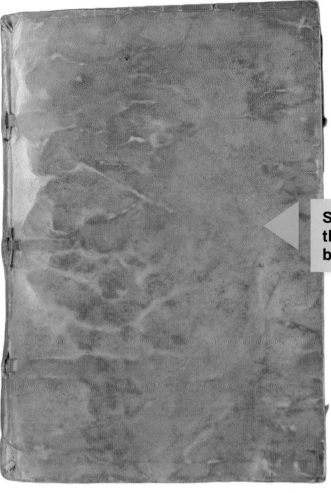

Some people believe the manuscript is a book about health.

Many people believe the writing uses a code. Several cryptographers have tried to crack it. Some have made guesses. But so far, no guesses have been proved.

WEIRD WORDS

Some people think the manuscript comes from an ancient civilization. It could use a language that no longer exists. Others say the language is just made up.

The book's text could use an anagram. This type of code mixes up the letters in each word.

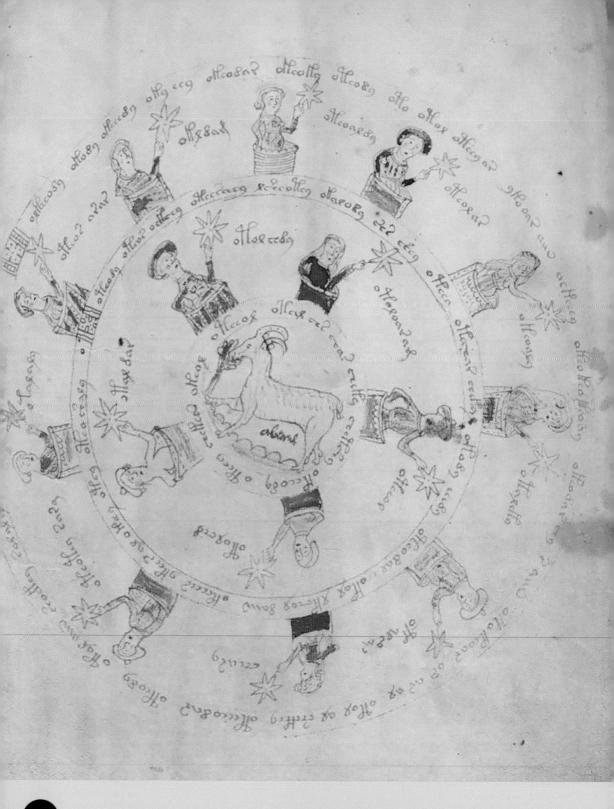

Scientists in Canada tried a new way of translating. They used a computer program. It found what a few words might mean. But the book's true meaning remains unknown.

FAST FACT

The book's strange language is sometimes called "Voynichese."

According to the computer program, one section contained words related to farming.

COMPREHENSION
QUESTIONS

Write your answers on a separate piece of paper.

1. Write a few sentences describing the main ideas of Chapter 3.

2. Do you think people will ever find out what the Voynich Manuscript means? Why or why not'?

3. When did Wilfrid Voynich buy the manuscript?

    A. in the 1400s

    B. in 1912

    C. in 2009

4. When was the manuscript probably written?

    A. in the 1400s

    B. in 1912

    C. in 2009

5. What does successful mean in this book?

Voynich tried to translate the strange words.
But he was not successful.

    A. able to do something
    B. wanting to try something
    C. afraid to do something

6. What does exists mean in this book?

Some people think the manuscript comes from
an ancient civilization. It could use a language
that no longer exists.

    A. happened long ago
    B. is still used
    C. will be used later

Answer key on page 32.

GLOSSARY

alchemy

A blend of magic and science that people used to try changing one type of material into another.

astronomy

The study of objects in space, such as planets and stars.

civilization

A large group of people with a shared history, culture, and government.

cosmology

The study of how the universe began and is structured.

cryptographers

People who study ways to create and solve codes.

manuscript

A book or other written text.

translate

To change something from one language to another.

vellum

Pages made from the skin of a cow.

TO LEARN MORE

BOOKS

Agrimbau, Diego. *Leonardo da Vinci*. North Mankato, MN:
  Capstone Press, 2018.

Hansen, Grace. *History's Ancient and Medieval Secrets*.
  Minneapolis: Abdo Publishing, 2022.

Thomas, Rachael L. *Classic Codes and Ciphers*.
  Minneapolis: Lerner Publications, 2022.

ONLINE RESOURCES

Visit www.apexeditions.com to find links and resources
related to this title.

ABOUT THE AUTHOR

Ashley Gish earned her degree in creative writing from
Minnesota State University, Mankato. She has authored more
than 60 juvenile nonfiction books. Ashley lives happily in
Rochester, Minnesota, with her husband, daughter, dog, cat,
and three chickens.

INDEX

ANSWER KEY:
1. Answers will vary; 2. Answers will vary; 3. B; 4. A; 5. A; 6. B